AF143913

BOOK ANALYSIS

By Stacie Bradly

Bleak House

BY CHARLES DICKENS

BOOK ANALYSIS

**Shed new light
on your favorite books with**

Bright
≡Summaries.com

www.brightsummaries.com

CHARLES DICKENS

- **Born in Portsmouth in 1812.**
- **Died in Gad's Hill, Kent in 1870.**
- **Notable works:**
  - *Oliver Twist* (1838), novel
  - *David Copperfield* (1850), novel
  - *Great Expectations* (1860-61), novel

Charles John Huffam Dickens was the second eldest of eight children born to Elizabeth and John Dickens. After his father's arrest when he was 12, Dickens began work at a blacking warehouse. Despite his lack of formal education, Dickens became a solicitor's clerk, then a reader at the British Museum, then a parliamentary reporter in 1832. In 1836 he married Catherine Hogarth, with whom he had ten children.

A prolific writer, he was published almost every year from 1833 until his death. He worked as an editor and journalist and was active both charitably and politically. Due to a long-standing affair, he separated from his wife in 1858 before beginning public reading tours. During the Staplehurst Rail Crash in 1865, Dickens helped to save and comfort passengers before returning for his manuscript of *Our Mutual Friend* (1865). He then revisited America, completing a book tour despite his deteriorating health. He returned to England the next year and continued his readings and publications before dying of a stroke in 1970. His body was buried in Poet's Corner in Westminster Abbey.

BLEAK HOUSE

A WEB OF REALISM

- **Genre:** serialised novel
- **Reference edition:** Dickens, C. (2003) *Bleak House.* London: Penguin Classics.
- **1st edition:** 1853
- **Themes:** law, justice, childhood, family values, secrets, realism, Victorian society

Bleak House was published in monthly instalments from 1852 to 1853. As Tracy suggests, *"Bleak House* was Dickens' most successful novel to date" (Paroissien, 2008: 380), and it is still one of his most famous novels. He used the novel to showcase the failings of Victorian society, namely its judicial system. He displays the hidden darkness behind a society which glorifies its technological and supposed societal advances.

The novel switches between first-person narration by the orphan Esther Summerson and a third person omniscient narrator. In doing so, Dickens presents an interesting juxtaposition of restrained politeness and thinly veiled contempt. He interweaves numerous subplots into a complex web of secrecy, blackmail, legal battles, and despair. This web touches on the concept of family, reputation, extreme poverty, justice, and so much more. What is overwhelmingly present throughout the entire novel, however, is a scathing indictment of the systems put in place to protect and serve the public.

SUMMARY

THE CASE

The novel opens in the Court of Chancery, which is dealing with the case of Jarndyce and Jarndyce. The lawsuit has been going on for so long that no one remembers how it started. At this point, it is only benefiting the lawyers. It is decided that a young boy and girl will go to live with their uncle. Mr Tulkinghorn visits Lady Dedlock and her husband, Sir Leicester, to update them on the case. Upon seeing some documents, Lady Dedlock asks who wrote them as the handwriting is nice. Mr Tulkinghorn says that he will enquire about it when suddenly Lady Dedlock becomes rather ill and has to leave.

A NEW BEGINNING

Esther Summerson is raised by her supposed godmother, Miss Barbary, believing her parents to be dead. When Miss Barbary dies suddenly, Esther is told that she will be going to live with a new guardian, Mr Jarndyce. She will be well provided for and educated to a high standard. Six years pass before she meets two young cousins, Richard Carstone and Ada Clare, who are beneficiaries of the Jarndyce case. They are all to live in Bleak House. As they start their journey, they meet an old woman who ominously suggests that judgement will come on the case. The group stay the night at the Jellybys', where they are surprised by the uncleanliness of the house and the general disarray of the family. Whilst on a walk the next day, the group meet the old woman from the day before. She decides to show them Chancery, which is actually a shop overladen with random items and legal papers. The shopkeeper is Krook, also known as the Lord Chancellor. He knows a lot about the Jarndyce case and copies out some letters from a Jarndyce letter even though he cannot read. After the old lady shows them her birdcages, the group leave before beginning their journey to Bleak House. On the way to Bleak House, the group receive letters from Mr Jarndyce requesting that they do not express gratitude for his help. Esther is given the housekeeping keys and is shocked to be given such a responsibility. A guest, Harold

Skimpole, arrives for dinner. Richard and Ada seem close and sing together at the piano before Richard disappears with Mr Skimpole. Richard calls for Esther and informs her that Harold is being arrested due to debt. They bail him out so that he does not have to go to Coavinses (a debtor's prison). Jarndyce orders them to never do so again.

A CURSE

At Chesney Wold, the housekeeper, Mrs Rouncewell, is visited by her grandson, Watt. Two men arrive and are taken on a tour of the house. One of the men, Mr Guppy, is entranced by the portrait of Lady Dedlock and swears that he knows her somehow. They are intrigued by the terrace called the Ghost's Walk, but Mrs Rouncewell will not explain why. After they leave, Mrs Rouncewell tells Rosa and Watt the tale: Lady Morbury Dedlock spied on her husband's meetings and relayed the information to King Charles's adversaries. After her husband's relative killed her beloved brother during battle, she began to hate her in-laws as well as the king. She tried to sabotage them by hurting their horses but when caught, she was badly lamed by her husband's horse. In an attempt to get better, she would walk along the terrace with her stick until one day, she collapsed. Before she died, she cursed the Dedlock family.

NEW FRIENDS?

Esther is shown the Growlery, the room Mr Jarndyce goes to when he needs to complain and feels an easterly wind. He tells her more about the Jarndyce case, namely that it is to do with a will and that the money has all been used up by the never-ending court case. It drove Tom Jarndyce, his uncle and the original owner of Bleak House, to suicide. Esther becomes responsible for much of Mr Jarndyce's correspondence and is visited by the demanding Mrs Pardiggle. She insists that Ada and Esther accompany her on her rounds where she preaches to hostile recipients. After she leaves, the girls try to help the people they have just met – a beaten woman, Jenny, and her baby. The girls leave and return later that night with Richard and food.

UNEXPECTED EVENTS

Richard and Ada are falling in love. Mr Jarndyce tries in vain to advance Richard's career as a sailor with Sir Dedlock. Lawrence Boythorn visits Bleak House and brings along his pet bird. The bird does not stay in a cage but on his head. Esther asks Mr Jarndyce if Boythorn is married. It turns out that he has never been married due to a broken heart long ago. The next day, Mr Guppy arrives looking for Boythorn. After his meeting, they have lunch and Mr Guppy proposes to Esther, who says no. Tulkinghorn visits the Snagsbys' house and tells Mr Snagsby that the recent Jarndyce papers were written very nicely. Upon enquiry, he is told that Nemo wrote them. The pair go to Krook's shop, where Nemo is supposed to live, and find Nemo dead, seemingly from an overdose. At the courthouse, Nemo's neighbours are questioned, though no one has any information. A young homeless boy named Jo says that Nemo was a friend who gave him money and a place to stay. At Chesney Wold, the Dedlocks have returned from Paris. Lady Dedlock is enchanted by Rosa's beauty, sending her maid, Hortense, into a fit of jealousy. Tulkinghorn arrives and discusses

Boythorn's lawsuit with him but makes no progress. He also informs Lady Dedlock of the writer, Nemo's, death.

A DOCTOR CALLS

Meanwhile, Richard decides to study medicine and Kenge is sorting out the logistics with Richard's cousin, Bayham Badger, with whom they all dine. Esther notices Mr Guppy following her and is unnerved by his continual presence. Ada and Richard express their "secret" love to Esther, who tells Jarndyce. They are happy but decide to proceed with caution. Esther was attracted to a young man at Badger's dinner. During a visit, Miss Jellyby says that she has been taking dancing lessons and has become secretly engaged to Mr Turveydrop. Esther goes to meet the Turveydrops with Miss Jellyby before calling upon the mad old woman, Miss Flite, from Krook's shop. Miss Flite has become unwell since Nemo's death and is treated by a doctor. Miss Flite's doctor, Mr Woodcourt, turns out to be Esther's crush from before. Skimpole's house has been taken by a debt collector. When looking for his debt collector, Neckett, Jarndyce and Esther find that he is dead, and that his three young children have been surviving on their own.

DÉJÀ VU

Jo is trying to get back to his home, Tom-all-Alone's, when he is approached by a woman who asks him about Nemo. After visiting his grave, she gives him money and disappears. Richard is unhappy in his new profession and changes course to study law. Mr Woodcourt leaves for Asia and covertly sends flowers to Esther. During a visit to Chesney Wold, Esther sees Lady Dedlock and has a sense of déjà vu. Later, Lady Dedlock's voice is mistaken for Esther's. When they are formally introduced, Lady Dedlock is reluctant to look at Esther and enquires about Jarndyce's familiarity with her estranged sister. A policeman tries to remove Jo from the area around Krook's shop, but he claims to know Mr Snagsby, who confirms it. Jo informs them of the woman who paid him for information about Nemo's death and many questions are asked before he manages to escape. Tulkinghorn introduces Snagsby to Inspector Bucket, who is investigating the death of Nemo. After talking with Jo, he discovers that the mysterious lady bribing Jo for information was wearing Hortense's clothing. Hortense quits her job.

AN EXPLOSIVE REVELATION

Charlotte Neckett, one of the orphans of the debt collector, becomes Esther's handmaid. Richard decides to join the army, leading Jarndyce to tell Ada that she should end their relationship. Tulkinghorn bribes George for a sample of Nemo's writing but is refused. Whilst visiting Lady Dedlock, Guppy reveals that he knows who her guardian was, who Esther's father was (Captain Hawdon), and that he was living under the alias of Nemo. Guppy goes to fetch some of his letters to prove it. Lady Dedlock cries as she realises that Esther is her daughter, whom she had believed to be dead. Esther visits Jenny and discovers Jo ill upon the floor. She takes him to Bleak House to nurse him, though he disappears, and she gets ill in the process. When Guppy arrives to search for Hawdon's letters at Krook's shop, he finds that Krook has spontaneously combusted. He gives up on the letters and tells Lady Dedlock that they no longer exist.

SCARRED

Esther is recovering from her smallpox and is told that a woman has been asking about her and took the handkerchief she mislaid. Also, her crush has returned from Asia. Esther goes to Boythorn's to recover and discovers that she has been scarred by the smallpox, marring her beauty. She is then told by Lady Dedlock that she is her daughter, but that it can never be spoken of and that they must never see each other again. Meanwhile, Richard is becoming so involved in the Jarndyce case that Jarndyce has stopped speaking to him. He has left the army and is solely focused on the case. Tulkinghorn suggests that he has discovered Lady Dedlock's secret. Hortense visits Tulkinghorn and, blaming him for her misfortune, wants him to find her a job. After he suggests that he will arrest her, she retreats. Telling Jarndyce that she has met her mother, Esther finds out that Boythorn was her aunt's sweetheart and that she broke his heart to raise her. Jarndyce then proposes to Esther through a letter, and she accepts. Mr Woodcourt runs into Jo, who tells him that a man at Bleak House scared him so much that he left. Woodcourt helps to find Jo new lodgings, but unfortunately he passes away.

A MURDER

Rosa is soon fired by Lady Dedlock in an attempt to preserve her reputation. This angers Tulkinghorn, who is subsequently murdered. Inspector Bucket arrests George for the murder. Despite this, he continues to investigate the case, finding Lady Dedlock's letters. After talking with Sir Leicester Dedlock, Bucket pieces everything together, arresting Hortense for the murder which she tried to pin on Lady Dedlock. As it turns out, George is Mrs Rouncewell's son whom she believed to be missing in action. Lady Dedlock runs away after finding out that her letters still exist. Sir Leicester suffers from a stroke and forgives his wife completely. Inspector Bucket and Esther go in search of Lady Dedlock, but they find her dead at the cemetery.

A RESOLUTION

Meanwhile, Richard and Ada have secretly married and Ada is pregnant. Richard has become ill from his obsession over the Jarndyce case. Mr Woodcourt declares his love for Esther once again, but she tells him that she is engaged. Esther begins to plan her wedding and visits Jarndyce while he is on a business trip to Yorkshire. Once there, he informs her that he has bought Woodcourt a house and that Esther should marry him and live there. The house is already decorated to her taste and has been named Bleak House. The estranged couple reunites. After the discovery of a new will, the Jarndyce case is over. No one inherits anything as the money is all gone. The news leads to Richard's death. Ada gives birth to a boy and raises him without his father, while Esther becomes a happy housewife and has two daughters with Woodcourt.

CHARACTER STUDY

ESTHER SUMMERSON

Esther is the novel's protagonist, and much of the story is told through her first-person narrative. While she often notes that she is not clever or does not believe herself capable, she shows herself to be a reliable and skilful narrator.

As a young orphan, she is raised by Miss Barbary, whom she believes to be her godmother. Miss Barbary is strict and unfeeling, bordering on emotionally abusive, which Esther believes to be a sign of virtue. She believes that she deserves what she gets and that she must make amends. She undervalues her talents and sees the good in everyone but herself. She is not allowed to celebrate her birthday and calls it "the most melancholy day at home, in the whole year" (p. 29). This leads her to wonder whether she killed her mother in childbirth. After Miss Barbary dies, Esther is taken into the care of Mr Jarndyce and is educated before moving to Bleak House. She takes on the running of Bleak House, is entrusted with the housekeeping keys, and deals with much of Jarndyce's correspondence. She is shown to be dependable and astute despite her self-depreciating instinct.

Throughout the novel, Esther is shown to be selfless, sweet, and caring, often helping those less fortunate than her. It is this tendency which leads her to contract smallpox from Jo, which subsequently scars her for life. During the course of the novel, it is discovered that Miss Barbary was actually her aunt, Lady Dedlock was her mother, and Captain Hawdon (Nemo) was her father. After a brief engagement to Mr Jarndyce, Esther marries Mr Woodcourt and has two children.

MR JOHN JARNDYCE

Mr Jarndyce is the proprietor of Bleak House and takes in the trio of orphans: Esther, Ada, and Richard. He is kind and selfless but hates to be thanked for his generosity. He is uncomfortable with emotions and generally tries to avoid such situations. He is superstitious and claims that an east wind is blowing any time he senses something bad. He relies heavily on Esther and admits that when he took her in, he hoped that she would later become his wife and the mistress of Bleak House. He proposes to Esther through a letter – once again avoiding an emotionally charged situation. Mr Jarndyce hates the case and wants nothing to do with it. He sees that it is corrupt, pointless, and damaging to those around him. His selflessness shines through when he buys a house for Mr Woodcourt out of gratitude, which he decorates for Esther. He releases her from their engagement so that she can be with the man she loves. He is humble and forgiving and takes in Ada after Richard's death, looking after her and her new-born son.

RICHARD CARSTONE

Richard is another orphan involved in the Jarndyce case and is taken in by Mr Jarndyce, along with his cousin Ada and Esther. He is flighty, unreliable, and weak-willed. He dislikes making decisions, preferring that others do it for him. He is not good with money and spends it like water or puts it into the Jarndyce case. He is quite similar to Harold Skimpole in this regard, though no one excuses him for it. He marries Ada in secret and says that he is pursuing the Jarndyce case for her. He anticipates a big pay-out when it is over and cannot think of anything else. He does not listen to anyone but his lawyer and ignores the signs that the court case has consumed all the money. It is the definitive news that there is no money left that kills him, leaving behind his wife Ada and their unborn child. He is a symbol for potential and domestic bliss thwarted by a corrupt, money-focused system.

ADA CLARE

Ada is beautiful, with long flowing golden hair. She is one of the orphans involved in the Jarndyce case and is taken into Mr Jarndyce's care. She is Esther's closest friend. She is very caring and even cries at the sight of an ill baby. She is well-educated and thoroughly accomplished in the creative arts. She plays the piano and sings, and it is there that her courtship with Richard begins. She marries Richard in secret and has his son. It is not a happy marriage, as Richard is consumed by the Jarndyce case.

HAROLD SKIMPOLE

Harold is described by Mr Jarndyce as a child, despite the fact that he is a father. He does not know much about the world and simply wants to be free without the constraints of societal law. Skimpole takes money from everyone to pay for his never-ending debts. He does not seem to care that he has debt collectors chasing him as he knows that someone will bail him out. This is excused due to his childish nature.

LADY DEDLOCK

Lady Dedlock is married to Sir Leicester Dedlock and lives with him at Chesney Wold. When she was younger, she was in love Captain Hawdon and gave birth to an illegitimate child, Esther, whom she believed to be dead. When she discovers that Esther is actually alive, she does not try to connect with her, fearing that she would ruin the Dedlock name. She is preoccupied with class and reputation and this keeps her from connecting with anyone. Due to these fears, she often disguises herself to seek information, bribes people, and eventually runs away. She dies on her way to her former lover's grave.

MR TULKINGHORN

Tulkinghorn is one of the main lawyers involved in the Jarndyce case. He consults the Dedlocks on any developments and pursues answers relentlessly. He is like a dog with a bone. When he discovers Lady Dedlock's secret, he blackmails her with it. He is murdered by Hortense.

INSPECTOR BUCKET

Bucket is the representation of the police force in the novel and is one of the first detectives in English Literature (Editors of the Encyclopaedia Britannica, 2016) He investigates the death of Nemo and Lady Dedlock (on Tulkinghorn's request). He collects information much like a bucket collects water and is key in solving Tulkinghorn's murder and Hortense's frame job.

THE JELLYBY FAMILY

The children and house are severely neglected by their mother, who focuses on her ventures in Africa. The eldest child, Caddy, hates her family and is forced to write letters for her mother's African employ. Caddy refuses to marry Mr

Quale and instead marries Prince Turveydrop, her dance teacher.

MADEMOISELLE HORTENSE

Hortense is Lady Dedlock's jealous maid who kills Tulkinghorn and frames Lady Dedlock for the murder.

LORD CHANCELLOR (KROOK)

Often referred to as the Lord Chancellor, Krook owns the Rag and Bottle Warehouse, also known as the Court of Chancery. He surrounds himself with legal documents and tries to copy them even though he cannot read or write. Later in the novel, he tries to teach himself to do so. He is also the landlord of Miss Flite and Nemo. He dies of spontaneous combustion.

MISS FLITE

Often seen as a mad old woman, Miss Flite is obsessed with the day of judgement for the Jarndyce case. She keeps around 20 birds that she will release on that day. She represents the large number of people trapped by the case awaiting release and brings a sense of impending doom to the story through her prophetic comments.

JO

Jo is a homeless orphan who is often paid for information. He passes smallpox to Esther and eventually dies of the disease.

NEMO

Nemo, also known as Captain Hawdon, was Lady Dedlock's former lover and Esther's father. He copied documents for the Jarndyce and Jarndyce case. He died from a supposed overdose.

ANALYSIS

THE COURT OF CHANCERY

If *Bleak House* revolves around a lawsuit, the Court of Chancery is at its centre. What is supposed to be the heart of the English judicial system and a symbol of justice and civilised society has been warped until it is almost unrecognisable. Cases are unending, expensive, and dragged on by money-grabbing lawyers excited for their next pay check. The only people who win are the lawyers, not the poor layman seeking what is rightfully theirs. Justice does not exist. In his early depictions of the court, Dickens described it as surrounded by the London fog:

> "...well may the fog hang heavy in it, as if it would never get out; well may the stained glass windows lose their colour, and admit no light of day into the place..." (p. 15)

Light becomes a symbol of truth and justice, something which is no longer found in the court. The systems put in place to highlight such truth have been tainted by the London fog of advancement, opportunism, and capitalism. The court is filled with an overwhelming darkness which corrupts any beauty to be found.

In Chapter Five, we are led to believe that Esther, Richard, and Ada are going to visit the court to meet the Lord Chancellor. However, they are as surprised as we are when they are instead led to Krook's Rag and Bottle shop, which is bursting at the seams with trinkets, miscellaneous items, and documents. Krook, an illiterate man with little education, is introduced as the Lord Chancellor. His explanation for the nicknames is that he owns a large amount of hair – a reference to the wigs worn in court at the time. Dickens suggests that the real Court of Chancery is embodied by this shop: piles of documents never to be read or investigated, goods wasting away upon the dusty shelves, no clear purpose to its arrangement. Furthermore, making use of the double meaning of the name, Dickens implies that the Lord Chancellor himself is a crook and that the court is run by an untrustworthy, money-grabbing criminal who breaks laws instead of enforcing them.

Moreover, Dickens implies that the corrupt lawyers are not necessarily acting of their own accord:

> "Eighteen of Mr Tangle's learned friends, each armed with a little summary of eighteen hundred sheets, bob up like eighteen hammers in a piano-forte, make eighteen bows, and drop into their eighteen places of obscurity." (p. 18)

They are part of a highly choreographed performance and nothing more. The hammers inside a piano are not in control of their actions. They are created to be manipulated and commanded at the press of a key. Much like these hammers, the lawyers are controlled by an outside force, a skilled musician who knows which keys to press, and when, to create the music that he wants to hear.

THE HOUSEHOLD AND MOTHERHOOD

When it comes to the depiction of the Victorian household, Dickens is second to none. As Waters suggests:

> "[Dickens] saw himself as a prophet of the hearth, and his contemporaries hailed his reputation as the purveyor of cosy domestic bliss. [...] Yet despite this reputation as the prophet of domestic bliss, any close examination of Dicken's novels reveals very few portraits of happy and harmonious families." (Waters, 2001: 120)

Bleak House could be seen as a pursuit of this ideal, perfect household. Dickens begins with the orphaned Esther, who lives with her godmother Miss Barbary. The house is quiet and joyless. Esther is not allowed to discuss her parents or celebrate special occasions. As a household, it is efficiently run; however, there is no love and sense of family, only an unnerving detachment from life. The next household comes in the form of the Jellybys. The Jellybys' house is dirty, manic, and neglected. Mrs Jellyby is so consumed by her business in Africa that she cannot see the potential happiness in front of her. She has rejected her maternal nature in favour of imperialism.

Next comes Mrs Pardiggle, a woman so obsessed by her virtuous reputation that she forces her children to give to charity and forces herself and her religion upon those she deems to need help. She even comments upon Mrs Jellyby's household:

> "I do not go with Mrs Jellyby in the treatment of her young family. It had been noticed. It has been observed that her young family are excluded from participation in the objects to which she is devoted. She may be right, she may be wrong; but, right or wrong, this is not my course with my young family. I take them everywhere." (p. 125)

Mrs Pardiggle sees the issues in the Jellyby household and admirably tries not to emulate them. What she does in the process, however, is go so far in the other direction that she is suffocating her household with her overbearing and forceful superiority complex. Dickens implies that, contrary to her own belief, her way is not the right way.

Throughout the novel, Esther observes the many different manners of running a household, and from a young age, she demonstrates the maternal impulse absent from the other families. By looking after every child, she can, for no compensation, running Bleak House smoothly, and aiding Mr Jarndyce and others in their affairs,

Esther becomes a symbol of the maternal instinct necessary to correctly run a household. At the end of the novel, Esther finally has her own children with her loving husband, Woodcourt. In her statement "we are not rich in the bank, but we have always prospered, and we have quite enough" (p. 988), it becomes clear that Esther has found a happy family, a contented household, and domestic bliss.

CHILDHOOD

A happy childhood is hard to come by in a Dickens novel. This is most likely because of his own childhood experiences. With his father's arrest in 1824, Dickens' childhood was ripped away from him. He was forced to go to work in terrible conditions and become the man of the house aged 12. It is therefore unsurprising that the theme of lost childhood became such a large part of his work. In *Bleak House*, the reader is faced with numerous children forced to grow up prematurely.

Firstly, there is Esther, who was emotionally abused by her aunt instead of being nurtured. She notes herself that she has a much different experience to the other girls in her class. She never had a childhood, she never had a family, and most of all, she did not have love. Upon her departure for Greenleaf, Esther decides to bury that part of her life:

> "A day or two before, I had wrapped the dear old doll in her own shawl, and quietly laid her – I am half ashamed to tell it – in the garden-earth, under the tree that shaded my old window." (p. 36)

The act of burying her doll symbolically eliminates any shred of childishness left in the young girl. In addition to this, however, the burial suggests that Esther is perhaps too familiar with death and loss for a young girl. Whilst sentimental, there is a pragmatism to her actions which suggests that she is more mature in this moment than many adults.

Dickens showcases the maturity of a child dragged into adulthood once again through the Neckett children:

> "The child he was nursing stretched forth its arms and cried out to be taken by Charley. The little girl took it, in a womanly sort of manner belonging to the apron and the bonnet, and

stood looking at us over the burden that clung to her most affectionately. [...] It was a thing to look at. The three children close together, and two of them relying solely on the third, and the third so young and yet with an air of age and steadiness that sat so strangely on the childish figure." (pp. 245-6)

Here Dickens portrays a 13-year-old girl as a mother. In the absence of a parental figure, Charley is forced to assume the responsibility for her younger siblings. Her strength is admirable, but it is tragic to imagine a child having to be the family's rock at such a young age. Thankfully, Esther is able to help the children by giving them jobs. One who cannot be helped is Jo, the poor street urchin, trodden on by all, and belonging to none. He is the epitome of Victorian poverty and cannot be saved. Throughout his life he has had to look after himself, though he never learned how. He is homeless, is often starved to the point of being unable to eat and relies on the kindness of others for food and shelter. In the end, he dies from pneumonia whilst searching for the light. Perhaps Mr Jarndyce puts it best when he states: "It is said that the children of the very poor are not brought up, but dragged up" (p. 88).

FURTHER REFLECTION

SOME QUESTIONS TO THINK ABOUT...

- To what extent could *Bleak House* be seen as a work of detective fiction? Explain your answer.
- In Latin, Nemo means no one. What significance does this bring to Captain Hawdon's character?
- What role does the supernatural play in the novel?
- How does the novel address the topics of scientific evidence and medicine?
- What is the purpose of having two different narrators?
- Explore the dynamics of female relationships in the novel.
- Examine the different settings in the novel: Bleak House, London, Chesney Wold, Tom-all-Alone's, etc.
- A large portion of the novel is spent travelling. What is the significance of these journeys?

We want to hear from you!
Leave a comment on your online library
and share your favourite books on social media!

FURTHER READING

REFERENCE EDITION

- Dickens, C. (2003) *Bleak House*. London: Penguin Classics.

REFERENCE STUDIES

- Butterworth, R. (2015) *Dickens, Religion and Society*. New York: Palgrave Macmillan.

- The Editors of Encyclopaedia Britannica. (2016) Inspector Bucket. *Encyclopædia Britannica, Inc.* [Online]. [Accessed 30 November 2018]. Available from: <https://www.britannica.com/topic/Inspector-Bucket>

- Jordan, J. O. (2001) *The Cambridge Companion to Charles Dickens*. Cambridge: Cambridge University Press.

- Paroissien, D. (2008) *A Companion to Charles Dickens*. Malden, MA: Blackwell Publishers.

ADDITIONAL SOURCES

- Douglas-Fairhurst, R. (2013) Why Should we Study Dickens? *University of Oxford*. [Online]. [Accessed 30 November 2018]. Available from: <https://podcasts.ox.ac.uk/why-should-we-study-dickens>

- Douglas-Fairhurst, R. (2012) Why Dickens? *University of Oxford.* [Online]. [Accessed 30 November 2018]. Available from: <https://podcasts.ox.ac.uk/why-dickens>

- Gill, S. (2012) Dickens' Railways. *University of Oxford.* [Online]. [Accessed 30 November 2018]. Available from: <https://podcasts.ox.ac.uk/dickens-railways>

- Jackson, A. et all. (2012) Rich and Poor in Britain in the Age of Dickens and Today. *University of Oxford.* [Online]. [Accessed 30 November 2018]. Available from: <https://podcasts.ox.ac.uk/rich-and-poor-britain-age-dickens-and-today-0>

ADAPTATIONS

- *Jo.* (1876) [Play] Written by John Pringle Burnett.

- *Bleak House.* (1920) [Silent film]. Maurice Elvey. Dir. UK: Ideal.

- *Bleak House.* (1959) [TV miniseries]. UK: BBC.

- *Bleak House.* (1985) [TV miniseries]. UK: BBC.

- *Bleak House.* (1998) [Radio series]. UK: BBC Radio 4.

- *Bleak House.* (2005) [TV miniseries]. UK: BBC.

MORE FROM BRIGHTSUMMARIES.COM

- Reading guide – *Great Expectations* by Charles Dickens.

- Reading guide – *Hard Times* by Charles Dickens.

- Reading guide – *Oliver Twist* by Charles Dickens.

BOOK ANALYSIS

Bright ≡Summaries.com

More guides to rediscover your love of literature

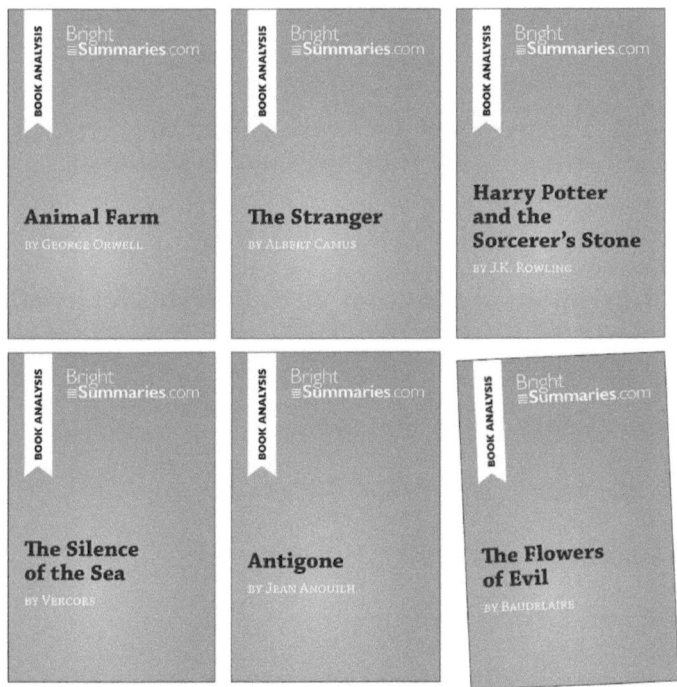

Animal Farm
BY GEORGE ORWELL

The Stranger
BY ALBERT CAMUS

Harry Potter and the Sorcerer's Stone
BY J.K. ROWLING

The Silence of the Sea
BY VERCORS

Antigone
BY JEAN ANOUILH

The Flowers of Evil
BY BAUDELAIRE

www.brightsummaries.com

Although the editor makes every effort to
verify the accuracy of the information published,
BrightSummaries.com accepts no responsibility for
the content of this book.

© BrightSummaries.com, 2019. All rights reserved.

www.brightsummaries.com

Ebook EAN: 9782808015837

Paperback EAN: 9782808015844

Legal Deposit: D/2018/12603/551

Cover: © Primento

Digital conception by Primento, the digital partner of
publishers.